ALGEBRA WARM-UPS

Short Exercises for Review and Exploration

Scott McFadden

DALE SEYMOUR PUBLICATIONS

Cover and illustrations: Mitchell Rose

ISBN 0-86651-344-2
Order number DS01712

DALE
SEYMOUR
PUBLICATIONS
P.O. BOX 10888
PALO ALTO, CA 94303

10 11 12 13 14 15-MA-95

CONTENTS

Preface

As a secondary mathematics teacher I am fully aware of the importance of giving students some kind of activity at the beginning of class. A *Warm-Up* activity, like those included in this book, can set the stage for the remainder of the period in addition to reviewing basic mathematical concepts. Also, a *Warm-Up* usually allows the teacher a few minutes of uninterrupted time to take care of those chores that seem to arise at the start of class.

There are not enough *Warm-Ups* to be used on a one-a-day basis. On other days, perhaps students can start with a challenge problem, some mental computation exercises, or a quiz.

Algebra Warm-Ups was more difficult to write than its predecessor, *Math Warm-Ups for Junior High.* This difficulty was not due to a lack of problems to include; rather, it was due to the placement of the problems. For example, some textbooks introduce functions and graphing very early, while others present this topic in the second semester. Thus, even though many problems in the *Warm-Ups* are intended to be introductory, you may wish to postpone some of them until you cover the topic in your lessons.

Good luck with the *Warm-Up* activities. They should provide your students with some good review as well as some challenging mathematical experiences.

Scott McFadden
Sheldon High School
Eugene, Oregon

INTRODUCTION

What is in *Algebra Warm-Ups?*

Algebra Warm-Ups contains 70 warm-up lessons. Each *Warm-Up* includes a set of five problems and an enrichment problem called a BONUS.

What are some special features of the *Warm-Ups?*

- Skill Maintenance—Students need frequent reviews of arithmetic and algebraic concepts and skills. The *Warm-Ups* provide this necessary skill maintenance and concept reinforcement.

- Concept Development—Although much of the content of the *Warm-Ups* is review, some exercises are designed to develop certain concepts. It is likely, however, that you will need to provide more concept development for most topics.

- Problem Solving—The bonus problems are intended to provide challenging problem solving experiences for all students. Many of the bonus problems can be easily extended fo further enrich these experiences. You may wish to use some of the extensions as the "problem of the week."

- Teacher Commentary—Answers and some comments are provided for each *Warm-Up*. Many of the comments are intended to stimulate discussion when you go over the problems in class.

What is the most distinguishing feature of the *Warm-Ups?*

- Problem Solving—Emphasis throughout the *Warm-Ups* is placed on the development and use of problem-solving strategies. Seven of the most important strategies are introduced in the bonus problems of the first lessons. These problem-solving strategies are reinforced throughout the remainder of the *Warm-Ups*. For more information and lessons on the development and use of problem-solving strategies, please refer to the book *Problem Solving in Mathematics—Algebra,* by the Lane County Mathematics Project, which is also available from Dale Seymour Publications.

For what level are the *Warm-Ups* intended?

- *Warm-Ups* can be used effectively with low achievers in algebra. Perhaps some of the exercises will need to be simplified and more time may be needed.

  The *Warm-Ups* can serve as an excellent diagnostic tool. You can easily provide additional practice when certain weaknesses are diagnosed.

- Many high achievers in algebra also need to have frequent review of mathematical concepts. The *Warm-Ups* provide this review. Also, the bonus problems are highly stimulating for advanced students.

How should the *Warm-Ups* be used?

- Enough *Warm-Ups* (70 in all) are included so you can use two of them each week.

- The *Warm-Ups* are short. Most can be done in about 10 minutes.

- *Warm-Ups* should be done at the beginning of the class period. They provide a good "warm-up" to the rest of the period's activities.

- Certain topics are developed and reinforced many times throughout the book. Thus, in most cases it is best if the *Warm-Ups* are done in the order in which they appear.

- *Warm-Ups* can easily be graded on a 5-point basis with an extra credit point given for the bonus. You may wish to include items similar to the *Warm-Ups* on your quizzes and tests.

WARM-UP 9

Identify which problem-solving strategy listed in the box would be best to use for each problem, then solve the problem.

1. $1 \cdot 8 + 1 =$ _____

$12 \cdot 8 + 2 =$ _____

$123 \cdot 8 + 3 =$ _____   Strategy: _____

Predict the answer to $1{,}234 \cdot 8 + 4$. Check your prediction. _____

*2. Use 3 darts. Each dart must hit the board. How many different scores are possible?

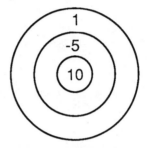

Strategy: _____

_____ scores

3. A 10-inch by 10-inch piece of cardboard has a 2-inch by 2-inch square cut out of each corner. The sides are then folded up to make a box without a lid. What is the volume of the box?

Volume: _____   Strategy: _____

4. The area of a square is 484 square inches. How long is each side? (No calculators allowed.)

Area: _____   Strategy: _____

5. Complete this sequence of numbers:

7.9, 6.8, 5.7, 4.6, ____, ____, ____, ____, ____   Strategy: _____

BONUS: Mr. Farmer raises ducks and cows. Solve these ducks-and-cows problems.

a. Mr. Farmer's animals have a total of 20 heads and 36 feet. How many ducks does he have? _____

b. Mr. Farmer's animals have a total of 20 heads and 84 feet. How many ducks does he have? _____

c. Mr. Farmer's animals have a total of 20 heads and 51 feet. How many ducks does he have? _____

WARM-UP 10

1. True or false?

    $5[-2 + (-10)] = 5 \cdot (-2) + 5 \cdot (-10)$ _____

2. Evaluate this expression for $a = -3$, $b = -4$, and $c = -5$.

    $a(b + c)$

    _____

3. Evaluate this expression for $a = -3$, $b = -4$, and $c = -5$.

    $ab + ac$

    _____

4. Use the *Look For A Pattern* strategy to help you complete this table.

1st	2nd	3rd	4th	5th	6th	7th	1,000th
3	5	7	9	11	13	15	

5. Multiply across and down to find the answers for the blank spaces.

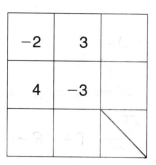

BONUS: *Working Backwards* is an important problem-solving strategy. See if you can solve this problem by working backwards.

Barbara is thinking of a number. If you multiply it by 5, then subtract 4, then add 6, and finally divide by 2, the result is 51. What number is Barbara thinking of?

_____20_____

WARM-UP 11

1. a. $(-1)^2 =$ _____

d. $(-1)^5 =$ _____

b. $(-1)^3 =$ _____

e. $(-1)^{25} =$ _____

c. $(-1)^4 =$ _____

f. $(-1)^{100} =$ _____

2. Multiply across and down to find the answers for the blank spaces.

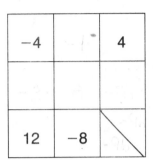

−4		4
12	−8	

3. Which of these expressions have the same answer? _____

    a. $5 - (3 - 4) =$ _____

    b. $5 - 3 - 4 =$ _____

    c. $5 - 3 + 4 =$ _____

4. Evaluate this expression for $a = -2$, $b = -3$, and $c = -5$.

$a(b - c)$

_____

5. Evaluate this expression for $a = -2$, $b = -3$, and $c = -5$.

$ab - ac$

_____

BONUS: See if you can solve this equation for n by using the *Working Backwards* strategy.

$$\frac{3n + 5}{2} - 6 = -1$$

$n =$ _____

WARM-UP 12

1. **a.** $|-3| - |-10| =$ _____

    b. $|23| + |-18| - |-2.5| =$ _____

2. Verify that $-3n + 5n = 2n$ by completing this table.

n	2	−2	0	10
Left side	4			
Right side	4			

3. Solve the following problem. Use the *Guess And Check* strategy if you like.

    The sum of two numbers is 88. The larger number is 16 more than the smaller number. What is the smaller number?

    _____

4. Solve for *n*.

    $\dfrac{3}{2}n = 1$ $n =$ _____

5. Solve for *b*.

    $\dfrac{2b - 3}{3} - 5 = 10$ $b =$ _____

★ **BONUS:** *Eliminate Possibilities* is an important problem-solving strategy.

Solve this problem by first eliminating some possible solutions.

$$\begin{array}{r} m\ m\ m \\ n\ n\ n \\ +\ r\ \ r\ \ r \\ \hline t\ \ t\ \ t \end{array}$$

The letters *m*, *n*, *r*, and *t* each represent a different whole number. Which of these numbers could be *t t t*? Circle your answer(s).

333   444   555   666   777

WARM-UP 13

1. Verify that $-m = -1m$ by completing this table.

m	3	-3	5	-5	0
Left side					
Right side					

2. Solve for n.

   $-3n + 2 = 23$ $n =$ _____

3. *Equivalent equations* are equations that have the same solution. Is this equation equivalent to the one you solved in Exercise 2? _____

   $n + 5 = 2n + 12$ $n =$ _____

4. Solve the following problem. Use the *Guess And Check* strategy if you like.

   The perimeter of a rectangle is 78 units. The length is 5 units more than the width. Find the length.

   _____

5. Solve for n.

   $-\dfrac{5}{7}n + 1 = 21$ $n =$ _____

BONUS: Solve the problem below by first eliminating some possible answers. Find the number:

- that is less than 100
- that is an odd number
- that is a multiple of 5
- that is divisible by 3
- whose digit sum is an odd number

_____

WARM-UP 14

1. Solve this problem. Use the *Guess And Check* strategy if you like.

   LeAnne has $4 in dimes and nickels. She has 10 more dimes than nickels. How many nickels does she have?

   _____

2. Solve for *m*.

   $5m + 2 = 3m + 2(m + 1)$

   $m =$ _____

3. Solve for *m*.

   $7(m - 4) = 7m - 3$

   $m =$ _____

4. Verify that $-n + 6n + (-2n) = 3n$ by replacing *n* with 10.

   _____

5. Write an equation that is equivalent (has the same solution) to the equation below.

   $3x + 4 = 10$

   _____

BONUS: Another important problem-solving strategy is to *Simplify The Problem*. Read the problem below, then use simpler cases to look for patterns.

Ten talkative teenagers decided to install their own telephone system. The system would connect each house with the other nine. How many wires do the teenagers need for their telephone network?

_____

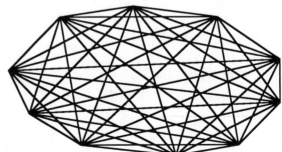

WARM-UP 15

1. Add across and down to find the
    answers for the blank spaces.

$-a$	$2a$	
$5a$	$-3a$	

2. Solve this problem. Use the *Guess And Check* strategy if you like.

    Lisa is twice as old as Shelly, and Shelly is 10 years older than Jeff. The sum of their ages is 50. How old is Jeff?

    _____

3. The following is an example of the *distributive property*.

    $-3[a + (-6)] = -3a + 18$

    Verify this property by replacing *a* with 10.

    _____

4. What values of *x* will satisfy this inequality?

    $x + 10 > 2$

    _____

5. Solve for *n*.

    $-2(n + 6) = -12 + -2n$

    $n =$ _____

BONUS: Solve the following problem by first *Simplifying The Problem*, then *Making A Systematic List*.

How many diagonals can be drawn inside an 8-sided figure?

_____

WARM-UP 16

Identify which problem-solving strategy listed in the box would be best to use for each problem, then solve the problem.

Simplify The Problem
Eliminate Possibilities
Work Backwards
Use A Drawing
Make A Systematic List
Look For A Pattern
Guess And Check

1. Jennifer made up this puzzle.

   I'm thinking of a number.
   First you add −5.
   Next, multiply by −2.
   Then subtract 6.
   Finally, divide by 2.

   What is the number if the final result is 5.5?

   Strategy: _____ _____

2. A rectangular field is 50 feet wide by 80 feet long. Fence posts are to be placed every 10 feet around the field. How many posts are needed?

   Strategy: _____ _____

3. Twelve people are at a party. Each person shakes hands with all the other people. What is the total number of handshakes?

   Strategy: _____ _____

4. How many ways can you make change for 25¢ using only pennies, nickels, and dimes?

   Strategy: _____ _____

5. Solve for *n*, to the nearest tenth. (No calculators allowed.)

   $n^2 = 82$

   Strategy: _____   *n* = _____

BONUS: *Pizza Puzzle*

Using four cuts, what is the greatest number of pieces of pizza you can get? The cuts have to be straight from edge to edge. (The answer is not 8.)

   Strategy: _____ _____

WARM-UP 17

1. Evaluate each expression for $x = -6$ and $y = -3$.

    a. $x + y =$ _____

    c. $xy =$ _____

    b. $x - y =$ _____

    d. $\dfrac{x}{y} =$ _____

2. Solve this problem. Use *Guess And Check* if you like.

A 79-inch rope is to be cut into two pieces. One piece is to be 19 inches longer than the other. How long is each piece?

_____

3. Simplify this expression by combining like terms. Verify your result by replacing *n* with -4.

$-n + 4n - 6n$

_____

4. What values of *y* will satisfy this inequality?

$3y + 2 < -7$

_____

5. Solve for *n*.

    $\dfrac{3}{2}n - 3 = 9$ $n =$ _____

BONUS: Study this pattern: 1, 5, 6, 11, 17, 28, 45

Notice that: $1 + 5 = 6$
                 $5 + 6 = 11$
                 $6 + 11 = 17$

This is called the *Adding Pattern*. Use the *Adding Pattern* to fill in the blanks.

a. 3, 4, 7, ____, ____, ____, ____

b. -3, ____, -2, ____, ____, ____, ____

c. 5, ____, ____, 9, ____, ____

WARM-UP 18

1. Simplify the following expression by combining like terms. Verify your result by replacing *a* with −3 and *b* with −4.

   $2a - b + 3a - 7b$

   _____

2. Solve for *n*.

   $5n + 2(n - 1) = -3 + 7n$

   $n =$ _____

3. Find an expression for the perimeter of this rectangle. Simplify your result.

   _____

   $8x - 4$

   $5x + 3$

4. The sum of three numbers is 73. The second number is twice as large as the first number. The third number is 8 more than the second number. What is the smallest number?

   _____

5. Solve for *n*.

   $n + 2n + (2n + 8) = 73$

   $n =$ _____

BONUS: This example demonstrates the *Adding Pattern*.

3, 4, 7, 11, 18, 29, …

Use the *Adding Pattern* to fill in the blanks.

a. 6, ____, ____, 4

b. 10, ____, ____, ____, ____, 0

WARM-UP 19

1. The length of a rectangle is 5 inches more than the width. The perimeter is 72 inches. What is the width?

   _____

2. Solve this equation for w.

   $2w + 2(w + 5) = 72$

   $w =$ _____

3. What values of n will satisfy this inequality? Be sure to check your result.

   $-5n + 1 < 26$

   $n =$ _____

4. Look for a pattern, then complete this table.

1	2	3	4	5	6	10	
1	4	9	16				361

5. Evaluate each expression for $x = 10$.

   a. $(5x)^2 =$ _____

   b. $5x^2 =$ _____

BONUS: Indicate which problem-solving strategy or strategies listed in the box would be best to use to solve the following problem, then solve the problem.

Mr. Ace, the tennis coach, needs to select a doubles team from his 10-person squad. How many different teams can he select?

Strategy: _____

_____

> *Simplify The Problem*
> *Eliminate Possibilities*
> *Work Backwards*
> *Use A Drawing*
> *Make A Systematic List*
> *Look For A Pattern*
> *Guess And Check*

WARM-UP 20

1. Evaluate each expression for $x = 3$.

    a. $(-2x)^3 =$ _____

    b. $-2x^3 =$ _____

2. True or false? If false, what is the correct result?

    $(-3n)^3 = -27n^3$

    _____

3. Find the width of this rectangle if the area is 165.

    _____

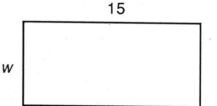

4. Simplify this expression. Check your result by replacing n with -3.

    $10n - (n - 8)$

    _____

5. The perimeter of a rectangle is 78. The length is twice the width. What is the width?

    _____

BONUS: Rectangular Numbers

```
 . .      . . .      . . . .      . . . .
          . . .      . . . .      . . . .
                     . . . .      . . . .
                                  . . . .
1st       2nd        3rd          4th
```

Look for patterns, then complete this table.

1st	2nd	3rd	4th	5th	6th	100th	nth
2	6	12	20				

1. True or false? If false, what is the correct result?

   $(2n^2)^3 = 6n^5$

   _____

2. Simplify this expression. Check your result by replacing x with -5.

   $5x - (2x - 4)$

   _____

3. Solve for n. Check your result.

   $5n - (2n - 4) = 28$

   $n = $ _____

4. These four numbers are called *consecutive numbers:*

   44, 45, 46, 47

   Find four consecutive numbers with a sum of 102.

   ____, ____, ____, ____

5. Solve for n.

   $n + (n + 1) + (n + 2) + (n + 3) = 102$

   $n = $ _____

BONUS: Triangular Numbers

1st   2nd   3rd   4th

Look for patterns, then complete this table.

1st	2nd	3rd	4th	5th	6th	100th	nth
1	3	6	10				

WARM-UP 22

1. Claude's math quiz required him to simplify each of the following expressions. Are his answers true or false? Substitute values to see.

   a. $(n^3) \cdot (n^2) = \underline{n^6}$ \hspace{1cm} _____

   b. $(n \cdot n \cdot n) \cdot (n \cdot n) = \underline{n^5}$ \hspace{1cm} _____

   c. $(2n)^3 = \underline{6n^3}$ \hspace{1cm} _____

   d. $(2n)(2n)(2n) = \underline{8n^3}$ \hspace{1cm} _____

2. These four numbers are *consecutive odd numbers*:

   15, 17, 19, 21

   Find four consecutive odd numbers with a sum of 200.

   _____, _____, _____, _____,

3. Solve for n.

   $n + (n + 2) + (n + 4) + (n + 6) = 200$

   $n = $ _____

4. Solve for n. Check your answer.

   $5n - (3n - 1) = 3$ \hspace{2cm} $n = $ _____

5. Solve for n. Check your answer.

   $5n + (3n - 1) = 3$ \hspace{2cm} $n = $ _____

BONUS: There are 8 teams in a basketball league. Each team plays every other team once. How many games are played altogether? What problem-solving strategies did you use?

_____

Strategy: _____

| Simplify The Problem |
| Eliminate Possibilities |
| Work Backwards |
| Use A Drawing |
| Make A Systematic List |
| Look For A Pattern |
| Guess And Check |

WARM-UP 23

1. Simplify this expression. Check your result by replacing n with 2.

   $(2n^3) \cdot (2n)^3$

   _____

2. The area of a square is 144 square inches. How long is each side?

   _____

3. A bottle and a cork cost $1.10. The bottle costs $1.00 more than the cork. How much does the cork cost?

   _____

4. Make up an equation that has a solution of 3. The unknown (n) must appear on both sides of the equation.

   _____

5. The following is an example of the *distributive property*.

   $a(b + c) = ab + ac$

   Use the distributive property to simplify this expression.

   $n(5n + 7)$

   _____

BONUS: Indicate which strategy or strategies from the list in the box would be best to use to solve this puzzle, then solve the problem.

Mr. Wheeler collects old bicycles and tricycles. In his collection there are 50 wheels and 23 seats. How many bicycles and how many tricycles does Mr. Wheeler have?

Strategy: _____

_____

| *Simplify The Problem* |
| *Eliminate Possibilities* |
| *Work Backwards* |
| *Use A Drawing* |
| *Make A Systematic List* |
| *Look For A Pattern* |
| *Guess And Check* |

1. Study this figure. The area of the figure can be represented by $n(n + 2)$. Use the distributive property to write this expression in another way.

_____

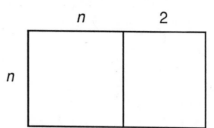

2. More information is needed to solve this puzzle. Make up additional information so that the puzzle can be solved, then solve your puzzle.

The second number is 8 larger than twice the first. How large is the first number?

_____

_____

3. Solve for n.

$3n + 15 = 2(n + 2) + n - 4$

$n =$ _____

4. Make up an equation that has no solution.

_____

5. Write all the whole number divisors (factors) of 48.

_____

BONUS: The area of a rectangle is 247. The width and length are both whole numbers greater than 1. What are the dimensions of the rectangle? (Hint: Use the *Eliminate Possibilities* strategy.)

_____

WARM-UP 25

1. This problem has too much information. Cross out the information that is not needed, then solve the problem.

   Margie is 16 years old. Her telephone number is 746-3310. She has been selling papers for 3 years. Last week she sold 5 more papers on Sunday than on Saturday. She sold a total of 73 papers for the two days. Papers cost 25 cents each. How many papers did Margie sell last Sunday?

   _____

2. Solve for n.

   $2(3n + 6) = 3(2n + 4)$

   $n =$ _____

3. Make up an equation that has an infinite number of solutions.

   _____

4. Give all the factors of 64.

   _____

5. Express the area of this rectangle in two different ways.

   _____

   _____

BONUS: What is the last digit of $2^{1,000}$?

   _____

WARM-UP 26

1. True or false? If false, what is the correct result?

$$\frac{x^8}{x^2} = x^6$$

_____

2. Find the missing factor.

$$\left(\boxed{}\right) \cdot (x^2y) = 2x^4y^3$$

3. The area of this rectangle can be expressed as $(x + 3) \cdot (x + 2)$. Write a different way to express the area by combining the areas of the rectangles.

_____

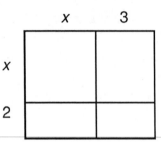

4. Write a story problem associated with this equation, then solve your problem.

$$x + (x + 2) + (x + 4) = 66$$

_____

_____

_____

5. Find two solutions.

$$x^2 + 1 = 50$$

$x =$ _____ $x =$ _____

BONUS: Use only the numbers below and any operations you like to find as many different whole number answers as possible.

$0, -2, 6$

_____

WARM-UP 27

1. Express the area of this rectangle in two different ways.

   _____

   _____

   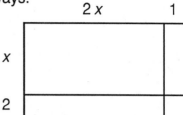

2. Simplify this expression. Check your result by replacing n with -2.

   $$\frac{n^6}{n^3}$$

   _____

3. Write a story problem associated with this figure. Then solve your problem.

   _____

   _____

   _____

   _____

   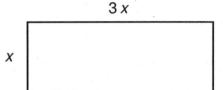

   Perimeter = 100 cm

4. $(-2xy^4)\left(\boxed{}\right) = 16xy^5z$

5. Solve for n.

   $$-\frac{3}{5}n + 1 = 4$$

   $n =$ _____

BONUS: Indicate which strategy from the list in the box would be best to use to solve this problem, then solve it.

Find the ages of three people.
Clue 1: The product of their ages is 96.
Clue 2: One person is a teenager.
There are 2 possible answers.

Strategy: _____

_____

Simplify The Problem
Eliminate Possibilities
Work Backwards
Use A Drawing
Make A Systematic List
Look For A Pattern
Guess And Check

WARM-UP 28

1. Which of Claude's answers in this quiz is correct?

   a. $\dfrac{n^6}{n^2} = n^3$ _____

   b. $\dfrac{n \cdot n \cdot n \cdot n \cdot n \cdot n}{n \cdot n} = n^4$ _____

   _____

2. Multiply. Check your result by replacing x with 10.

   $(x + 5)(x + 3)$

   _____

3. Jennifer is twice as old as Matt, and Matt is 7 years older than Kevin. The sum of their ages is 53. How old is Kevin?

   _____

4. Solve for x.

   $x + (x + 7) + 2(x + 7) = 53$

   $x =$ _____

5. $(-5 - 3)^2 + (-1)^5 =$ _____

BONUS: Julie made up a problem.

Choose a number. Add 3. Multiply by 2. Add 4. Divide by 2. Subtract your original number.

Julie says your answer is 5. Is she correct? Try this trick with other numbers. Use algebra to show why this works.

_____

1. Multiply. Check your result by replacing y with -3.

   $(y + 5)(y - 4)$

   _____

2. Solve for n.

   $5n + 10(n + 7) = 400$

   $n =$ _____

3. Jeff has \$4 in dimes and nickels. He has 7 more dimes than nickels. How many nickels does he have?

   _____

4. Fill in the correct power of ten.

   $5{,}300{,}000{,}000 = 5.3 \times 10^{\boxed{}}$

5. $\dfrac{(-2)^5}{2^3} + \dfrac{2^5}{(-2)^3} =$ _____

BONUS: Pick your favorite number. Double it. Add 6. Subtract 18. Multiply by 2. Divide by 4. Add 6.

What answer do you get? Will this work for other numbers? Use algebra to show why the trick works.

_____

WARM-UP 30

1. Solve for n.

$(4.0 \times 10^6)(2.1 \times 10^7) = 8.4 \times 10^n$

$n =$ _____

2. Lynn has $5.40 in quarters and dimes. She has two more quarters than dimes. How many dimes does she have?

_____

3. Multiply. Check your result by replacing x with -3.

$(2x + 3)(x - 1)$

_____

4. Find three fractions between $\frac{1}{4}$ and $\frac{1}{3}$.

____, ____, ____

5. Simplify this expression by combining like terms.

$5a - 3b + 4a + 2(a - b)$

_____

BONUS: Pick a number. Add the number of months in a year. Subtract the number of days in a week. Multiply by 3. Subtract 15. Divide by 3. Will this work for any number? Use algebra to show why the trick works.

_____

WARM-UP 31

1. True or false? If false, what is the correct result?

$$\frac{(3.0 \cdot 10^4)(1.4 \cdot 10^8)}{(2.1 \cdot 10^3)} = 2.0 \cdot 10^4$$

_____

2. The area of a particular rectangle is expressed as $3n + 12$. Find an expression for this rectangle's length if its width is 3. (Use a drawing to help you.)

_____

3. Find the missing factor.

   $10n + 25 = (\boxed{})(2n + 5)$

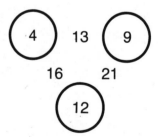

4. Solve for n.

   $2n + 3(10 - n) = 26$

   $n =$ _____

5. Steve bought 10 baseballs—some at $2 each and the rest at $3 each. How many $2 baseballs did he buy if he paid $26 for his purchase?

_____

BONUS: Notice that the numbers in these circles have been added to give the numbers between the circles.

What numbers should be put in the circles below? Use the *Guess And Check* strategy.

a.

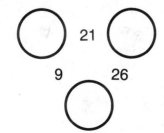

b.

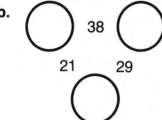

WARM-UP 32

1. Solve for x.

$$10^x \cdot 10^x = 10^{16}$$

$x = $ _____

2. Alan sold 30 tickets—some at \$3 each and the rest at \$4 each. How many \$3 tickets did he sell if his total sales amounted to \$100?

_____

3. Find the missing factor.

$$10a^2 + 30a = \left(\boxed{}\right)(2a + 6)$$

4. How long will it take Stacy to bicycle from a to b if she averages 12 miles per hour?

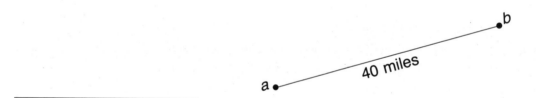

_____

5. Complete this table. Look for patterns.

1st	2nd	3rd	4th	5th	6th	100th	nth
10	21	32	43	54	65		

BONUS: The numbers that belong in the circles, when added, give the numbers between the circles. Use the *Guess And Check* strategy to fill in the blank circles.

a.

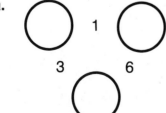

b.

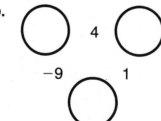

WARM-UP 33

1. The area of each smaller rectangle is given. Find an expression for the length and an expression for the width of the entire rectangle.

   Length: _____

   Width: _____

n^2	$3n$
$2n$	6

2. The area of a certain rectangle is expressed as $n^2 + 7n + 12$. Find an expression for the length and an expression for the width of this rectangle. (Use a drawing to help you.)

   Length: _____

   Width: _____

3. Solve for t.

   $15t + 12t = 108$

   $t =$ _____

4. Two bicyclists leave at the same time and same point and ride in opposite directions. James averages 15 miles per hour and Robert averages 12 miles per hour. In how many hours will they be 108 miles apart?

   _____

5. Solve for n.

   $$\frac{10^8}{10^n} = 10^6$$

   $n =$ _____

BONUS: The numbers that belong in the circles, when added, give the numbers between the circles. Use the *Guess And Check* strategy to fill in the blank circles.

$$\bigcirc \quad 5 \quad \bigcirc$$
$$-7 \qquad 9$$
$$\bigcirc$$

WARM-UP 34

1. Find both factors. Check your result by replacing n with 5.

$$(\boxed{})(\boxed{}) = n^2 - 10n + 16$$

2. Two long–distance runners leave at the same time and same point and run in opposite directions. Julie averages 10 miles per hour and Jenny averages 8 miles per hour. In how many hours will they be 27 miles apart?

_____

3. Evaluate this expression for $n = 4$.

$$\frac{n + 14}{n + 2}$$

$n = $ _____

4. True or false?

$$\frac{\cancel{n} + 14}{\cancel{n} + 2} = 7$$

_____

5. Write an expression for the nth term.

1st	2nd	3rd	4th	5th	6th	nth
5	9	13	17	21	25	

BONUS: Indicate which strategies from the list in the box would be best to solve this problem, then solve the problem.

| Simplify The Problem |
| Eliminate Possibilities |
| Work Backwards |
| Use A Drawing |
| Make A Systematic List |
| Look For A Pattern |
| Guess And Check |

Fig. 1   Fig. 2   Fig. 3

Figure 1 contains one angle.
Figure 2 contains three angles.
Figure 3 contains six angles.
If this procedure is continued,
how many angles would there be in:

a. Figure 4? _____   **c.** Figure 10? _____

b. Figure 5? _____   Strategies: _____

1. True or false?

$$\frac{n^2 + 2}{n^2} = 2$$

_____

2. Solve for n.

$6(n + 7) - 4n = 60$

$n =$ _____

3. Solve for x. There are two different solutions.

$(x + 3)(x - 8) = 0$

$x =$ _____

$x =$ _____

4. Solve for x. There are two different solutions.

$x^2 - 5x - 24 = 0$

$x =$ _____

$x =$ _____

5. The capacities of two trucks are 4 tons and 6 tons. The larger truck makes 7 more trips than the smaller one and delivers 60 more tons of freight per day. How many trips does the smaller truck make each day?

_____

BONUS: Slim was ordering a meal. He had the following choices:

1st Course	2nd Course	3rd Course
Soup	Beef	Pie
Salad	Lamb	Ice Cream
	Chicken	Cake
	Liver	

How many different 3-course meals could Slim order? (Use the _Make A Systematic List_ strategy.)

_____

WARM-UP 36

1. Did Claude simplify these expressions correctly on his quiz?

   a. $\dfrac{2}{3} \cdot \dfrac{(x+1)}{(x+1)} = \dfrac{2x+2}{3x+3}$

   _____

   b. $\dfrac{2x+2}{3x+3} = \dfrac{2}{3}$

   _____

2. Simplify this expression if possible.

   $\dfrac{4x+4}{5x+5}$

   _____

3. A large cake is cut into 4 pieces so that each slice is twice as heavy as the preceding one. If the entire cake weighs 5 pounds, how much does the smallest piece weigh?

   _____

4. Find both solutions to this equation.

   $x^2 - 7x + 10 = 0$

   $x =$ _____ $x =$ _____

5. Write an equation that has both -3 and -4 as solutions.

   _____

BONUS: Use only the numbers -1 to -5 to fill in the blank circles. The sum in each direction must be the same. Find three different sums.

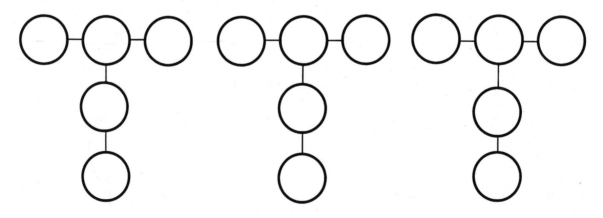

Sum: _____   Sum: _____   Sum: _____

1. Solve for n.

$$6n - 3(n + 27) = 9$$

$n =$ _____

2. Show why Claude's solution to this simplification problem is incorrect.

$$\frac{5 + \not{n}}{4 + \not{n}} = \frac{5}{4}$$

_____

3. Simplify these expressions if possible.

a. $\dfrac{5n}{10n}$ **b.** $\dfrac{5 + n}{10 + n}$

_____   _____

4. True or false?

a. $\dfrac{2}{3} + \dfrac{3}{4} = \dfrac{5}{7}$ **b.** $\dfrac{2}{3} + \dfrac{3}{4} = \dfrac{17}{12}$

_____   _____

5. The difference of two numbers is 27. If three times the larger number is subtracted from six times the smaller number, the difference is 9. Find the smaller number.

_____

BONUS: Use only the odd numbers 1, 3, 5, 7, 9, and 11 to fill in the blank circles. The sum in each direction must be the same.

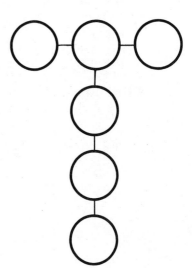

WARM-UP 38

1. Simplify this expression.

$$\frac{3n}{4} \cdot \frac{4}{9n}$$

_____

2. Write these fractions with a common denominator.

$$\frac{x}{3} \qquad \frac{x}{4}$$

_____

3. Simplify this expression.

$$\frac{x}{3} + \frac{x}{4}$$

_____

4. The formula for the area of a square is $a = s^2$. Complete this table.

s	1	2	3	4	5	6	17		
a	1	4	9					400	1,225

5. The sum of the angles of a triangle is always 180°. Suppose that two angles of a triangle are equal and the third angle is 5° less than each of the other two angles. How large is each angle?

_____

BONUS: The dimensions of a packing box are represented as $(n + 1)$, $(n + 2)$, and $(2n - 1)$. Each edge of the box will be fastened with packing tape. Write the simplest expression for the total amount of tape needed. (Hint: Use the _Make A Drawing_ strategy.)

_____

WARM-UP 39

1. Simplify this expression.

$$\frac{a}{2} + \frac{a}{3} + \frac{a}{4}$$

_____

2. Simplify this expression.

$$\frac{2a}{b} \cdot \frac{b^2}{6a^2}$$

_____

3. The formula for the circumference of a circle is $c = \pi d$. Using this formula, complete the table below. Use 3.1 as the value for π.

d	1	2	3	4	10	20	
c	3.1	6.2					77.5

4. Find the perimeter of this rectangle in simplest form.

$2x + 1$

x

_____

5. Find the area of the rectangle in Exercise 4 in simplest form.

_____

BONUS: Notice the pattern in the problem below, and find the final answer. (Hint: Take simpler cases.)

$$\left(1 - \tfrac{1}{2}\right)\left(1 - \tfrac{1}{3}\right)\left(1 - \tfrac{1}{4}\right) \cdots \left(1 - \tfrac{1}{99}\right)\left(1 - \tfrac{1}{100}\right) = _____$$

WARM-UP 40

1. Show the result of multiplying both sides of this equation by 12.

$$\frac{x}{3} + \frac{x}{4} = 7$$

_____

2. Solve for x.

$$4x + 3x = 84$$

$$x = \underline{\hspace{2cm}}$$

3. Use only the numbers 3, 6, 2, and 9 to write four different proportions. One has been done for you.

$$\frac{2}{6} = \frac{3}{9}$$

_____   _____

_____   _____

4. Richard's car averages 27 miles per gallon of gasoline. Use the formula $d = 27g$ to complete this table.

g	1	2	3	4	5	6	15	
d	27	54	81					810

5. $(-1)^{50} \cdot (-1)^{49} = \underline{\hspace{2cm}}$

BONUS: My father is 44 years old. My dog is 7 years old. If my dog were a human, he would be 56. If my father were a dog, how old would he be?

_____

WARM-UP 41

1. Use only the numbers 9, 4, 3, and 12 to write four different proportions.

   _____   _____   _____   _____

2. Which of the following ratios are equivalent to $\frac{35}{40}$? Circle your answer(s).

   $\frac{14}{16}$ $\frac{5}{6}$ $\frac{7}{8}$ $\frac{63}{72}$

3. Show the result of multiplying both sides of this equation by 24.

   $$\frac{2x}{3} - \frac{x}{4} = \frac{1}{24}$$

   _____

4. Solve for x.

   $$\frac{2x}{3} - \frac{x}{4} = \frac{1}{24}$$ $x =$ _____

5. The formula $d = \frac{1}{5}s$ tells you how many miles you are from a flash of lightning, where s is the number of seconds between seeing the lightning and hearing the thunder. Complete this table.

s	1	3	5	10	
d	$\frac{1}{5}$				$3\frac{1}{5}$

BONUS: Use only the numbers 1, 2, and 4 and any operation you like to find as many different whole number answers as possible. Two examples are:

$(1 + 2) \cdot 4 = 12$

$1 + 2 \cdot 4 = 9$

_____

WARM-UP 42

1. How far does a car travel after the driver hits the brakes before it stops? This formula gives a reasonably correct answer.

   $d = 0.055r^2$

   d = distance in feet
   r = speed of the car in miles per hour

   Complete this table.

r	10	20	30	60	80
d					

2. $(2x + 1)(2x - 1) =$ _____

3. $9x^2 - 1 = ($ [　　] $)($ [　　] $)$

4. Solve for x.

   $\dfrac{x}{3} - \dfrac{x}{9} = 2$

   $x =$ _____

5. Solve for n.

   $\dfrac{15}{25} = \dfrac{6}{n}$

   $n =$ _____

BONUS: Jenny had a party. Everyone at the party shook hands with everyone else. How many people were at the party if there were 78 handshakes?

_____

WARM-UP 43

1. Solve for *n*.

$$\frac{155}{5} = \frac{n}{8}$$

n = _____

2. Bryan can type 155 words in 5 minutes. At this rate, how many words can he type in 8 minutes?

_____

3. Simplify these expressions.

a. $(a - b)(a + b)$

_____

c. $39 \cdot 41$

_____

b. $(30 - 1)(30 + 1)$

_____

4. Slim loves hamburgers. This table shows how many he eats and the total cost. Complete the table.

Hamburgers (h)	5	10	15	20
Cost (c)	$4.45			

5. Write a formula that shows the cost of Slim's hamburgers.

_____

BONUS: This problem is from an old mathematics textbook published in 1863. In a certain school $\frac{1}{3}$ of the scholars were studying arithmetic, $\frac{1}{4}$ algebra, $\frac{1}{6}$ geometry, and the remainder, 18, were studying grammar. How many scholars were in the school?

_____

1. A 4-foot steel pipe weighs 15 pounds. How much will a similar pipe weigh if it is 7 feet long?

   _____

2. Write a story problem that is associated with this proportion, then solve your problem.

   $$\frac{5}{\$21} = \frac{12}{n}$$

   _____

   _____

   _____

3. This table shows how inexpensive gasoline was in 1970. Complete the table.

Gallons (g)	3	6	10	15	
Cost (c)	$1.05				$7.00

4. Write a formula that shows the cost of gasoline in 1970.

   _____

5. Solve for n.

   $$0.08n + 0.12n = 5$$

   $n =$ _____

BONUS: Christopher has 40 yards of fencing to use in building a pen for his dog. What are the dimensions of the pen that will provide the greatest room (area) for his dog? (Hint: Make a systematic list.)

_____

1. "Air Ball" Budd has made only 5 out of 19 free throws. What percent is this?

   _____

2. Write a story problem that is associated with this proportion, then solve your problem.

   $\dfrac{15}{16} = \dfrac{n}{100}$ _____

   _____

   _____

3. Solve for y. Check your solution.

   $2y + 5 < -3$

   $y = $ _____

4. Solve for y. Check your solution.

   $-2y + 5 < -3$

   $y = $ _____

5. This table shows a direct variation. Complete the table according to the pattern, then write a formula that fits the data.

x	0	2	5	8	10	15
y	0	5	12.5	20		

   _____

BONUS: Indicate which strategy or strategies from the list in the box would be best to use to solve the following puzzle, then solve the puzzle.

I'm thinking of a number.
If you add 3, then subtract 6, then divide by 2, and finally multiply by 4, the result is -8.
What is the number?

Strategy: _____

_____

| *Simplify The Problem* |
| *Eliminate Possibilities* |
| *Work Backwards* |
| *Use A Drawing* |
| *Make A Systematic List* |
| *Look For A Pattern* |
| *Guess And Check* |

WARM-UP 46

1. Mrs. Morris earns a commission of $175 on sales of $3,000. How much commission does she earn on sales of $6,500?

   _____

2. A car travels 30 miles per hour for 6 hours. How many hours does it take to travel the same distance at 40 miles per hour?

   _____

3. Solve for *b*. Check your solution.

   $-3b + 1 > 7$

   $b =$ _____

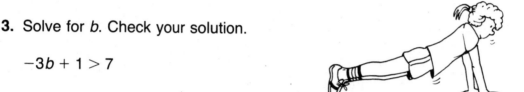

4. Simplify this expression.

   $$\frac{12 - 18}{-2} - (-3)^2$$

   _____

5. The coordinates of three vertices of a rectangle are (2,3), (2,8), and (10,3). What are the coordinates of the fourth vertex?

   _____

BONUS: Use four 4s and any of the four operations to make the numbers 1 through 10.

Example: $1 = \dfrac{4 + 4}{4 + 4}$

1 = _____   6 = _____

2 = _____   7 = _____

3 = _____   8 = _____

4 = _____   9 = _____

5 = _____   10 = _____

WARM-UP 47

1. Use these clues to draw this graph.

   - The graph is a straight line.
   - It goes through the origin (0,0).
   - It goes through (−2,3).

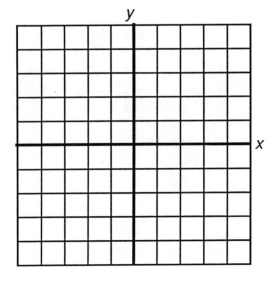

2. Draw this graph on the same grid.

   - The graph is a vertical line.
   - It crosses the x-axis (horizontal axis) at (3,0).

3. $\dfrac{n^2 + n}{n + 1}$

   Evaluate this expression for:

   a. $n = 4$ _____

   b. $n = -3$ _____

   c. $n = 10$ _____

4. Solve for n.

   $5n - (2n + 3) = 3$

   $n = $ _____

5. Solve this equation. Check your answer by replacing x with 6.

   $(x + 1)^2 = $ _____

BONUS: The coordinates of three vertices of a certain parallelogram are (5,2), (2,6), and (10,9).

a. Give the coordinates of a fourth vertex. _____

b. Give the coordinates of another point that could be the fourth vertex. _____

WARM-UP 48

1. Cross out the clue that is not needed in order to draw this graph.

   - The graph is a straight line.
   - It slopes sharply up from lower left to upper right.
   - It passes through $(-1,-5)$ and $(1,7)$.

2. Solve for n.

   $$n^2 + (n + 1)^2 = 365$$

   $n = $ _____

3. $\dfrac{n^2 - 1}{n - 1}$

   Evaluate this expression for:

   a. $n = 3$ _____

   b. $n = 4$ _____

   c. $n = 5$ _____

4. On a particular blueprint, 3 centimeters represents 10 feet. How long is a line that represents 15 feet?

   _____

5. The sum of the squares of two consecutive numbers is 365. Find the numbers.

   _____

BONUS:

This triangular grid has 3 units on a side. It contains 9 small triangles. How many small triangles are in a triangular grid that has 20 units on a side?

_____

WARM-UP 49

1. Use these clues to decide where these two graphs will intersect.

   - Both graphs are straight lines.
   - One graph is horizontal; the other is vertical.
   - One graph crosses the x-axis at -3; the other graph crosses the y-axis at -4.

   _____

2. What values of n make the denominator in this expression 0?

   $$\frac{5}{n^2 - 16}$$

   _____

3. Solve for n.

   $$\frac{n}{5} + \frac{n}{4} = \frac{1}{2} \qquad n = \text{_____}$$

4. Simplify this expresion.

   $$(2x)^3(3x)^2$$

   _____

5. If 2 men can paint a house in 3 days, how long will it take 4 men to paint the same house?

   _____

BONUS:

Matt got $1 on his first birthday.

On his second birthday he will get the amount from his previous birthday plus as many dollars as he is years old.

On his third birthday he gets the amount from his previous birthday plus as many dollars as he is years old.

If this pattern continues, how much will Matt receive on his 12th birthday?

_____

WARM-UP 50

1. The sum of the numbers x and y is 10. Complete the table of values that shows this relationship.

x	0	1	6		15		
y	10			-1		0	-2

2. Write a description of the graph suggested by the pairs of numbers in Exercise 1.

   _____

   _____

3. Find both solutions to this equation.

   $(2x + 1)(x - 5) = 0$

   $x =$ _____ $x =$ _____

4. Find both solutions to this equation.

   $2x^2 - 9x - 5 = 0$

   $x =$ _____ $x =$ _____

5. Julie competes in the long jump event. If Julie can jump 17 feet with a 10-yard run, how far can she jump with a 20-yard run?

   _____

BONUS:

Indicate which strategy or strategies from the list in the box would be best to use to solve the problems, then solve them.

If it takes 27 cubes to fill a cubical box:

a. How many cubes will be touching the bottom of the box?

   _____

b. How many cubes will be touching the sides?

   _____

Strategy: _____

> Simplify The Problem
> Eliminate Possibilities
> Work Backwards
> Use A Drawing
> Make A Systematic List
> Look For A Pattern
> Guess And Check

1. $y = 4x - 1$

Complete the table of values for this equation.

x	-2	-1	0	1	2	3
y						

2. Write a description of the graph suggested by the pairs of numbers in Exercise 1.

_____

_____

3. Which answer is correct? _____

a. $\dfrac{x}{3} + \dfrac{x}{5} = \dfrac{2x}{8}$

b. $\dfrac{x}{3} + \dfrac{x}{5} = \dfrac{x^2}{15}$

c. $\dfrac{x}{3} + \dfrac{x}{5} = \dfrac{8x}{15}$

4. Solve this puzzle. Carol is twice as old as Jane. Five years ago she was 3 times as old as Jane. How old is Jane?

_____

5. Solve for n.

$3(n - 5) = 2n - 5$

$n =$ _____

BONUS: Eight points are placed on a circle. How many lines are possible if each point is connected to each of the other points?

_____

1. $y = 2x + 6$

If this equation was graphed, where would the graph cross:

a. the y-axis? _____

b. the x-axis? _____

2. $xy = 12$

If this equation was graphed, where would the graph cross:

a. the y-axis? _____

b. the x-axis? _____

3. Nancy is six times as old as Mary. When will she be only twice as old as Mary?

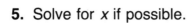

4. Solve for x if possible.

$x^2 - 5x - 24 = 0$

$x =$ _____

5. Solve for x if possible.

$x^2 - 8x + 24 = 0$

$x =$ _____

BONUS: This problem is from an algebra textbook written in 1887.

A fish was caught whose tail weighed 9 pounds. His head weighed as much as his tail and half his body, and his body weighed as much as his head and tail. How much did the fish weigh?

_____

WARM-UP 53

1. Where do the graphs of the following equations intersect?

   $x + y = 4$ $\qquad\qquad$ $x - y = 2$

   _____

2. Write two equations whose graphs intersect at the origin (0,0).

   _____

   _____

3. Complete this pattern.

   $10^3 = 1,000$

   $10^2 = 100$

   $10^1 =$ _____

   $10^0 =$ _____

   $10^{-1} =$ _____

   $10^{-2} =$ _____

   $10^{-3} =$ _____

4. According to the pattern in Exercise 3, find:

   a. $10^{-4} =$ _____

   b. $10^{-6} =$ _____

5. Simplify this expression. Check your answer by replacing x with 3.

   $$\frac{4x}{3} - \frac{x-1}{3}$$ $\qquad$ _____

BONUS: "Dead Eye" Joe is usually a good free throw shooter. Yet, he's made only 8 out of 20 free throws during the first part of the basketball season. How many consecutive successful shots must he make to raise his record to 60%?

_____

WARM-UP 54

1. Write two equations whose graphs each pass through (3,4).

   _____

   _____

2. Where do the graphs of these equations intersect?

   $x + 0 \cdot y = 3$

   $0 \cdot x + y = 4$

   _____

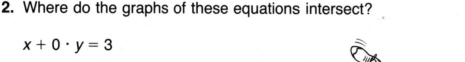

3. Solve for n.

   $3.1 \cdot 10^n = 0.000031$

   $n =$ _____

4. Solve for n.

   $2.1 \cdot 10^{-3} \cdot 4 \cdot 10^{-5} = 8.4 \cdot 10^n$

   $n =$ _____

5. Solve this puzzle.

   I'm thinking of two numbers. Their sum is 20, and their difference is 6. What are the numbers?

   _____

BONUS: "Air Ball" Budd is a terrible free throw shooter. Yet, he's done quite well during the first part of the basketball season, making 10 out of 16 free throws. How many consecutive free throws must "Air Ball" Budd miss to lower his record to 40%?

   _____

WARM-UP 55

1. Where do the graphs of these equations intersect?

$3x + y = 4$

$x + y = 2$

_____

2. Write an equation that results from adding the two equations in Exercise 1.

_____

Does this equation also pass through (1,1)? _____

3. Solve for n.

$2 \cdot 10^{-3} \cdot 3 \cdot 10^4 \cdot 8 \cdot 10^{-1} = 4.8 \cdot 10^n$

$n =$ _____

4. Evaluate this expression for $a = -2$.

$2a^3 \cdot (2a)^3$

_____

5. Solve this puzzle.

I'm thinking of two numbers. Their sum is 10. If you add the first number to twice the second number, the result is 8. What are the numbers?

_____

BONUS: The dimensions of a packing box are 10 inches by 15 inches by 20 inches. Each edge of the box will be fastened with packing tape. How many inches of tape are needed? (Hint: Use the *Make A Drawing* strategy.)

_____

WARM-UP 56

1. Solve this puzzle.

I'm thinking of two numbers. The first number added to the second number is 5. Twice the first number added to twice the second number is 10. What are the numbers?

_____

2. Where do the graphs of the following equations intersect?

$x + y = 5$

$2x + 2y = 10$

_____

3. This formula can be used to change a Fahrenheit temperature to a Celsius temperature.

$$C = \frac{5}{9}(F - 32)$$

Find C for:

a. $F = 32$ _____   **b.** $F = 41$ _____   **c.** $F = 23$ _____

4. Solve for n.

$2n + 3(n + 1) = -2$ $n =$ _____

5. Solve for n.

$2n - 3(n + 1) = -7$ $n =$ _____

BONUS: Indicate which strategy from the list in the box would be best to use to solve this problem, then solve it.

"Dead Eye" Joe made 15 points in a basketball game. 3 points are given for a "long shot," 2 points are given for a field goal, and 1 point is given for a free throw. In how many ways can "Dead Eye" score 15 points?

Strategy: _____

_____

| Simplify The Problem |
| Eliminate Possibilities |
| Work Backwards |
| Use A Drawing |
| Make A Systematic List |
| Look For A Pattern |
| Guess And Check |

WARM-UP 57

1. This formula can be used to change a Celsius temperature to a Fahrenheit temperature. Use it to help you complete this table.

   $F = \dfrac{9}{5} C + 32$

C	0	10	20	30	40	50
F						

2. Without graphing the formula in Exercise 1, can you tell whether the graph will be a straight line or a curved line? Explain your answer.

   _____

   _____

3. Write a number puzzle that is associated with these equations. Then solve your puzzle.

   $x + y = 10$ _____

   $x + 2y = 8$ _____

   _____

4. Complete this pattern.

   $-16, -8, -4, -2, -1,$ ____, ____, ____, ____

5. Solve for x. Check your solution.

   $3x - 1 > x + 3$ $x =$ _____

BONUS: You may use a calculator to help you solve this problem.

Write a 3-digit number. Write the same 3 digits after the number so you have a 6-digit number; for example, 352,352. Divide the new number by 13. Divide your answer by 11. Divide this new answer by 7.

Comment on your result. Explain why the puzzle works.

_____

_____

WARM-UP 58

1. The area of a certain rectangle is 24. Complete the table showing possible lengths and widths of this rectangle.

l	1	2	3	4	6	8	12	24
w								

2. Describe the graph of $lw = 24$.

   Will the graph ever touch the l-axis? _____

   Will the graph ever touch the w-axis? _____

3. Solve for x.

   $$4x - 15 = 2(x + 1)$$

   $x =$ _____

4. Write an expression for the area and the perimeter of this square.

   $2x + 1$

   Area: _____

   Perimeter: _____

5. Write an equation for this table of values.

x	1	2	3	4	5
y	−6	−6	−6	−6	−6

_____

BONUS: The dimensions of a 20-foot by 50-foot garden are to be increased by equal amounts. The new area will be increased by 1,800 square feet. Find the dimensions of the new garden. (Hint: First make a drawing and then write an equation that could be used to solve this problem.)

_____

1. Which height–weight formula do you feel is the best one? Explain your answer.

h = height in inches
w = weight in pounds

$w = 5h - 190$ $w = 180 - h$ $w = 2(h - 8)$

_____

2. Complete the diagram to show the result of multiplying $(x + 3) \cdot (x + 3)$.

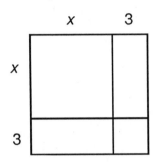

3. $2x^2 - x - 3 = (\boxed{})(\boxed{})$

4. $(2x^2 - x - 3) \div (x + 1) = $ _____

5. Solve for y.

$3(y - 2) = 2(y - 3)$

$y = $ _____

BONUS: Amy wants to travel from Elmtown to Lakeside at an average speed of 50 miles per hour. She travels half the distance and discovers that her average speed has been only 25 miles per hour. How fast must she drive for the remaining part of the trip if she is to average 50 miles per hour for the entire trip?

_____

WARM-UP 60

1. Write an expression for the area of this square's shaded region. The formula for the area of a circle is $a = \pi r^2$.

_____

2. Which equation(s) will have a graph that is a curved line?

$y = 2x + 1$ $y = x^2$ $xy = 24$

_____

3. Multiply.

$x(x + 1)(x + 2) =$ _____

4. Find all three solutions.

$x^3 + 3x^2 + 2x = 0$

$x =$ _____ $x =$ _____ $x =$ _____

5. Use the distributive property to write an expression equivalent to $2x(3x^2 + 5)$.

_____

BONUS: Indicate which strategy or strategies from the list in the box would be best to use to solve this problem, then solve the problem.

How many cubes would be needed to build the 10th figure?

```
Simplify The Problem
Eliminate Possibilities
Work Backwards
Use A Drawing
Make A Systematic List
Look For A Pattern
Guess And Check
```

  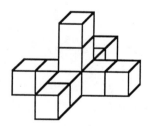

Strategy: _____

_____

1. Write an expression for the area of the shaded region.

   _____

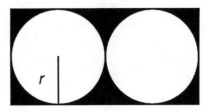

2. Use the distributive property to solve these problems mentally.

   a. $73 \cdot 89 + 73 \cdot 11 =$ _____

   b. $139 \cdot 75 + 139 \cdot 25 =$ _____

3. If these equations were graphed, which line would be steepest (have the greatest slope)?

   $y = 5x$ $y = 2x + 6$ $y = x - 3$

   _____

4. Solve for n, if possible.

   $2n^2 - n - 2 = 0$

   $n =$ _____

5. Matt has a small car. It used only 5 gallons of gasoline to travel 190 miles. At that rate, how far will it go on 12 gallons?

   _____

BONUS: Jill made two 6-sided dice and labeled each of them with these numbers:

$-3, -2, -1, 0, 1, 2.$

Suppose this pair of dice was tossed 1,000 times and the numbers on the two top faces were added. Which sum would probably be the most common? Why?

_____

WARM-UP 62

1. Write an expression for the area of this figure. _____

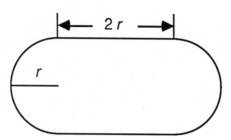

2. Solve this equation for y in terms of x.

   $2y - 4x = 7$

   $y = $ _____

3. Simplify each expression.

   a. $(5x + 2) + (2x - 3)$ _____

   b. $(5x + 2) - (2x - 3)$ _____

4. Pick a number. Multiply by 2. Subtract 8. Divide by 2. Add 4. What is the result? Use algebra to show why the trick works.

   _____

5. Solve for n.

   $3n - 2 = 5(n + 1) - 2n$

   $n = $ _____

BONUS: Find a 2-digit number whose square ends in the same 2-digit number. (Find more than one answer.)

_____

WARM-UP 63

1. Write an equation that is represented by each line shown.

   a _____

   b _____

   c _____

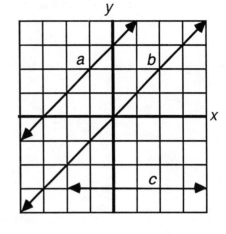

2. Simplify.

   $|-13 - 4| + (-2)^3$

   _____

3. Solve for x and y.

   $x + y = 7$

   $2x - y = 5$

   $x =$ _____

   $y =$ _____

4. Julie scored 19 out of 22 on a math test. Scores over 90% earn an A. Did Julie earn an A?

   _____

5. Solve for y in terms of x.

   $-2x + 3y = 1$

   $y =$ _____

BONUS: This problem is from a mathematics book published in 1880.

If a horse trots 3 miles in 8 minutes and 15 seconds, how far can he trot in an hour at the same rate?

_____

WARM-UP 64

1. Suppose the following equations were graphed. Describe any properties common to all three graphs.

   $$y = 2x - 3 \qquad y = -2x - 3 \qquad y = \frac{1}{2}x - 3$$

   _____

2. Solve for x and y.

   $$y = 2x - 3$$

   $$y = -2x - 3$$

   $$x = \underline{\hspace{2cm}}$$

   $$y = \underline{\hspace{2cm}}$$

3. Simplify. First, factor both the numerator and denominator.

   $$\frac{x^2 + 3x + 2}{x^2 + x}$$

   _____

4. Is Claude's answer to this problem true or false? (Substitute some numbers for x to find out.)

   $$(x + 6)^2 = \underline{x^2 + 36}$$

   _____

5. In Mr. Lopez's class, a person needs 90% to earn an A. Mr. Lopez gave a test containing 35 items. How many correct answers are necessary to receive an A?

   _____

BONUS: Apartments on the 10th floor of the Twin Towers Apartment Complex rent for $390 per month. Apartments on the 15th floor rent for $440 per month. At this rate, how much will it cost to rent an apartment on the 34th floor?

_____

WARM-UP 65

1. This formula relates the age of a person to hours of sleep.

   $h = (34 - a) \div 2$

   - Does the formula seem to work for you? _____

   - Does the formula seem to work for babies? _____

   - Does the formula seem to work for older people? _____

   - For what ages does the formula work best? _____

2. Solve for x and y.

   $y = -4x$ $x =$ _____

   $x - 2y = 9$ $y =$ _____

3. Solve for x and y.

   $x - 3y = -4$ $x =$ _____

   $2x + y = 6$ $y =$ _____

4. Simplify.

   $(x + 1)^2 + (x + 2)^2$

   _____

5. Solve for n.

   $\dfrac{10^n \cdot 10^6}{10^2} = 10^3$ $n =$ _____

BONUS: In this puzzle each different letter represents a different digit. What are the digits?

```
    S E N D
+   M O R E
---------
  M O N E Y
```

+ _____

_____

_____

WARM-UP 66

1. Crickets are remarkable in their ability to indicate the temperature. Use this formula to complete the table of values.

$$t = \frac{1}{4}c + 37$$

c = number of chirps per minute
t = temperature in degrees Fahrenheit

c	60	72	84	96	108
t					

2. A certain kind of ant can also be used as a thermometer. Use the formula to complete this table of values.

$$t = 11s + 39$$

s = speed in inches per minute
t = temperature in degrees Fahrenheit

s	1	2	3	4	5
t					

3. If a cricket chirps 108 times per minute, what is the approximate speed of the ant?

_____

4. Simplify.

$$-2x \cdot 3x^2 \cdot 4x^3$$

_____

5. Simplify.

$$|-2(3 - 5)| - |5 - 12|$$

_____

BONUS: If 3 cats can catch 3 rats in 3 minutes, how many cats are needed to catch 100 rats in 100 minutes?

_____

WARM-UP 67

1. Complete the table using this formula to find the distance an object falls.

$d = 16t^2$ t = the number of seconds d = the distance in feet

t	0	1	2	3	4	5
d						

2. Sketch the graph of the formula in Exercise 1.

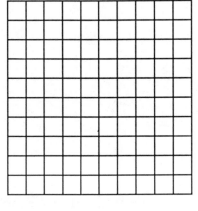

3. Suppose two objects of different weight are dropped. Will they reach the ground at the same time? Try it by dropping a coin and a book.

_____

4. Solve this equation for x in terms of y.

$y = 11x + 39$ $x =$ _____

5. Simplify.

$(n + 1)^2 - (n - 1)^2$ _____

BONUS: The local hardware store sells three types of window panes:

Corner panes   Edge panes   Center panes

The 3-foot by 5-foot window shown uses 4 corner panes, 8 edge panes, and 3 center panes. How many of each window pane type is used in these windows?

a. 3-foot by 6-foot _____

b. 3-foot by 10-foot _____

c. 3-foot by 100-foot _____

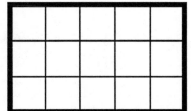

WARM-UP 68

Review of Graphing

1. Where do the graphs of these equations intersect?

$$x - y = 3 \qquad\qquad x + y = -3$$

_____

2. Write an equation for the graph shown.

_____

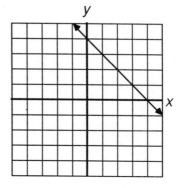

3. Suppose the following equations were graphed. Describe any properties common to each graph.

$$x + y = 3 \qquad y + 0 \cdot x = 3 \qquad y = x + 3$$

_____

4. Which, if any, of the following equations have curved line graphs?

$$y = x + 3 \qquad xy = 12 \qquad y = x^2 \qquad x - y = 3$$

_____

5. The coordinates of three vertices of a certain rectangle are $(0,0)$, $(2,-3)$, and $(-6,-4)$. What are the coordinates of the fourth vertex?

_____

BONUS: Sketch the graph of this equation.

$$|x| + |y| = 6$$

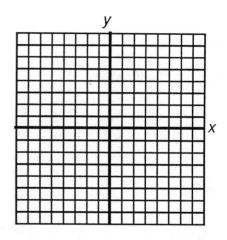

WARM-UP 69

Review of Equation Solving

1. $5x + 2(x - 3) = -6$

$x = $ _____

2. $2x - 3(x + 1) = x + 3$

$x = $ _____

3. $\dfrac{x}{2} + \dfrac{x}{3} = \dfrac{1}{6}$

$x = $ _____

4. $x^2 + 2x - 15 = 0$

$x = $ _____

5. Solve for x and y.

$2x - y = 0$

$4x - y = 14$

$x = $ _____

$y = $ _____

BONUS: $\dfrac{2x}{5} + \dfrac{x + 1}{2} = 8 - \dfrac{x - 1}{10}$

$x = $ _____

Review of Story Problems

Translate each problem to an equation or a pair of equations, then solve the problem.

1. The sum of three consecutive odd numbers is 255. What are the numbers?

_____

2. Two bicyclists begin at the same point and travel in opposite directions. One bicyclist rides at the rate of 20 miles per hour; the other rides at the rate of 10 miles per hour. In how many hours will they be 120 miles apart?

_____

3. Robin is half as old as Rich, and Robin is four years younger than Joan. The sum of their ages is 80. How old is Robin?

_____

4. Four cans of cat food and 3 cans of dog food cost $1.99. Four cans of the same cat food and 1 can of the same dog food cost $1.33. What is the cost of one can of cat food?

_____

5. The sum of two numbers is 20. The larger number exceeds twice the smaller number by 14. What are the two numbers?

_____

BONUS: This problem is from a French mathematics book. Can you solve it?

Une lampe électrique a consommé 120 watt-heures d'électricité en 15 heures. Combien d'en consomme t'elle en 50 heures?

_____

TEACHER'S COMMENTARY

A note about the Bonus problems: In many cases, more than one answer is possible. Please check student answers carefully, since students may find solutions other than those listed here and still be correct.

WARM-UP 1

1. 36
2. 35.8 cm
3. 180   *Emphasize order of operations.*
4. 5⅛
5. $15.00   *This problem can be done mentally.*

BONUS: 8 ducks, 12 cows

Encourage all students to do the Bonus Problems in Warm-Ups 1 through 15. These introduce and reinforce problem-solving strategies that can be used frequently in later problems. You may wish to start a bulletin board display that lists each problem-solving strategy as it is introduced. See Problem Solving in Mathematics—Algebra, *written by the Lane County Mathematics Project, for more problems that can be solved by using this strategy. This book is also available from Dale Seymour Publications.*

WARM-UP 2

1. 6   *Emphasize that this problem can be solved by the* Guess And Check *strategy.*

2. 306

3. 306   *The answers to Exercises 2 and 3 are the same due to the distributive property. Hopefully, students will recognize this and apply the property to similar problems occurring later.*

4. $p = l + w + l + w$

   $p = 2(l + w)$

   $p = 2l + 2w$

5. 38 cm

BONUS: 12

WARM-UP 3

1. 25   *Emphasize that the problem can be solved by using the* Guess And Check *strategy.*

2. 0   *Point out that multiplication by 0 always results in 0.*

3. 90

4. 200

5. 200   *The answers to Exercises 4 and 5 are the same due to the distributive property. Of course, Exercise 5 is much easier to work.*

BONUS:

  a. 2, 9, 16, 23, <u>30</u>, <u>37</u>, <u>44</u>

  b. 1, 3, 6, 10, <u>15</u>, <u>21</u>, <u>28</u>

  c. 14, 10, 6, 2, <u>−2</u>, <u>−6</u>, <u>−10</u>

  d. 1, 2, 6, 24, 120, <u>720</u>, <u>5,040</u>, <u>40,320</u>

Refer to Problem Solving in Mathematics—Algebra *for more problems that use* Look For A Pattern *and other problem-solving strategies.*

WARM-UP 4

1. **a.** 90   *Emphasize order of operations.*
   b. 180
2. 118
3. $11.76
4. $11.76   *Exercises 3 and 4 show the distributive property.*
5. −8.5°, −8°, −7.5°, 0°, 3°, 8°

BONUS: 9, 16, 25, 36, 100, 10,000

WARM-UP 5

1. $1^5, 3^2, 2^4, 4^3$

71

2.

Cuts	1	2	3	4	5	10	19
Pieces	2	4	6	8	10	20	38

3. 17   *This problem provides practice in using the* Guess And Check *strategy.*

4.

5. a. 65

 b. 65

 c. 35

 d. 35

BONUS: 12 ways   *It's important that students use a Systematic List like this one.*

d	n	p
2	1	0
2	0	5
1	3	0
1	2	5
1	1	10
1	0	15
0	5	0
0	4	5
0	3	10
0	2	15
0	1	20
0	0	25

WARM-UP 6

1.

29	15	44
13	47	60
42	62	104 / 104

Students may be surprised that the final answers are the same. Perhaps they could

try to find a set of numbers that does not give the same answers. (Of course, this is not possible, but students should be allowed to discover this on their own.)

2. a. 5°

 b. −25°

 c. 0°

3. 0

4. Undefined   *These problems provide an opportunity to show why, for example,* 0 ÷ 10 *is 0 and* 10 ÷ 0 *is undefined.*

5. 35

BONUS: 10 ways

q	d	n
2	0	0
1	2	1
1	1	3
1	0	5
0	5	0
0	4	2
0	3	4
0	2	6
0	1	8
0	0	10

WARM-UP 7

1.

−2	5	3
10	−4	6
8	1	9 / 9

Perhaps students can discover why the final answers are the same, regardless of the numbers used.

2. +2   *Emphasize that the sum of a number and its opposite is 0.*

72

3. $a = 21.5$ *See* Problem Solving in Mathematics—Algebra *to see how* Guess And Check *procedures are used to introduce equation solving.*

4. $b = 13$

5. 16.5

BONUS: 12 cubes   *Twelve cubes have paint on exactly two faces. These appear on the edges of the original cube.*

WARM-UP 8

1.

−3	2	−1
−6	5	−1
−9	7	−2 / −2

2. $n = 1$

3. $r = 2$

4. 15, 14, 12, 9, 5, <u>0</u>, <u>−6</u>, <u>−13</u>

5. True, because −4 is less than −2.

BONUS:
Area of the sidewalk is 74 square yards.

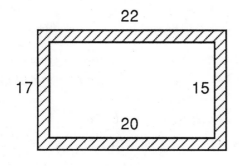

WARM-UP 9

1. *Look For A Pattern*

$$1 \cdot 8 + 1 = 9$$
$$12 \cdot 8 + 2 = 98$$
$$123 \cdot 8 + 3 = 987$$
$$1{,}234 \cdot 8 + 4 = 9{,}876$$

2. *Make A Systematic List*

10 different scores

10	−5	1	Total
✓✓✓			30
✓✓	✓		15
✓✓		✓	21
✓	✓✓		0
✓	✓	✓	6
✓		✓✓	12
	✓✓✓		−15
	✓✓	✓	− 9
	✓	✓✓	− 3
		✓✓✓	3

3. *Use A Drawing*

Volume is 72 cubic inches.

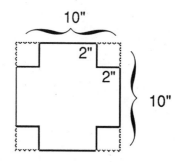

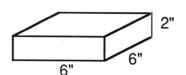

4. *Guess And Check*

22 inches

5. *Look For A Pattern*

7.9, 6.8, 5.7, 4.6, <u>3.5</u>, <u>2.4</u>, <u>1.3</u>, <u>0.2</u>, <u>−0.9</u>

BONUS: *Guess And Check*

   a. Not possible

   b. Not possible

   c. Not possible

Discuss why each of these problems is impossible to solve.

WARM-UP 10

1. True   *This is an example of the distributive property.*

2. 27

3. 27   *The answers to Exercises 2 and 3 are the same due to the distributive property.*

4. The pattern is 2n + 1.

1	2	3	4	5	6	7	1,000
3	5	7	9	11	13	15	2,001

5. *Remind students to multiply throughout the entire problem.*

-2	3	-6
4	-3	-12
-8	-9	72 / 72

BONUS: $(51 \cdot 2 - 6 + 4) \div 5 = \underline{20}$

WARM-UP 11

1. a. 1

   b. -1

   c. 1

   d. -1

   e. -1

   f. 1

2.

-4	-1	4
-3	8	-24
12	-8	-96 / -96

3. Exercises **a** and **c** have the same answer.

   a. 6   *Note the minus sign in front of the parentheses and how this affects the result.*

   b. -2

   c. 6

4. -4

5. -4

BONUS: $n = \frac{5}{3}$

WARM-UP 12

1. a. -7

   b. 38.5

2.

n	2	-2	0	10
Left side	4	-4	0	20
Right side	4	-4	0	20

3. 36   *Refer to the book* Problem Solving in Mathematics— Algebra *to see how* Guess And Check *procedures are used to introduce word problems.*

4. $n = \frac{2}{3}$ *Point out that the product of a number and its reciprocal is equal to 1.*

5. $b = 24$

BONUS: *t t t* can be either 666 or 777.

WARM-UP 13

1. Review this important property:
$-n = -1n$.

m	3	-3	5	-5	0
Left side	-3	3	-5	5	0
Right side	-3	3	-5	5	0

2. $n = -7$

3. Yes, both equations have a solution of -7.

4. 22 units

5. $n = -28$ *The multiplicative inverse is helpful in solving this equation:*

$$-\frac{5}{7}n + 1 = 21$$

$$-\frac{5}{7}n = 20$$

$$\left(-\frac{7}{5}\right)\left(-\frac{5}{7}n\right) = 20 \cdot \left(-\frac{7}{5}\right)$$

$$1n = -28$$

BONUS: 45

WARM-UP 14

1. 20 nickels

2. $m = $ any number

3. The equation has no solution.

> *It is important for students to recognize that some equations have an infinite number of solutions (Exercise 2) and some equations have no solution (Exercise 3).*

4. $-10 + 60 + (-20) = 30$

5. Any equation with a solution of 2 is equivalent to the given equation.

BONUS: *By taking simpler cases and extending the pattern we find that 45 wires are needed. It is important that this procedure is shown to your students.*

Persons	2	3	4	5	6	7	8	9	10
Wires	1	3	6	10	15	21	28	36	45

WARM-UP 15

1.

$-a$	$2a$	a
$5a$	$-3a$	$2a$
$4a$	$-a$	$3a$ / $3a$

2. Jeff is 5 years old.

3. $-3.4 = -30 + 18$

4. $x > -8$

5. $n = $ any number

BONUS:

Number of sides	3	4	5	6	7	8
Number of diagonals	0	2	5	9	14	22

WARM-UP 16

1. *Work Backwards*

$$\frac{5.5 \cdot 2 + 6}{-2} + (-5) = -3.5$$

2. *Use A Drawing*

26 posts

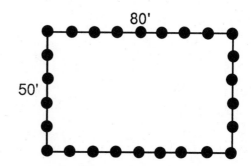

3. Several strategies are possible:
- *Take Simpler Cases*
- *Make Drawings*
- *Look For Patterns*

66 handshakes

People	2	3	4	5	6	7	8	9	10	11	12
Handshakes	1	3	6	10	15	21	28	36	45	55	66

4. *Make A Systematic List*

12 ways

d	n	p
2	1	0
2	0	5
1	3	0
1	2	5
1	1	10
1	0	15
0	5	0
0	4	5
0	3	10
0	2	15
0	1	20
0	0	25

5. *Guess And Check*

$n = 9.1$

BONUS: *Use A Drawing*

11 pieces

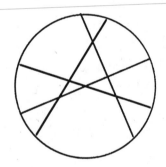

WARM-UP 17

1. a. -9

   b. -3

   c. 18

   d. 2

2. 30 inches and 49 inches

3. $-3n$

4. $y < -3$

5. $n = 8$

  BONUS: a. 3, 4, 7, <u>11</u>, <u>18</u>, <u>29</u>, <u>47</u>

       b. -3, <u>1</u>, -2, <u>-1</u>, <u>-3</u>, <u>-4</u>, <u>-7</u>

       c. 5, <u>2</u>, <u>7</u>, 9, <u>16</u>, <u>25</u>

WARM-UP 18

1. $5a - 8b$

2. No solution possible

3. $26x - 2$

4. 13

5. $n = 13$ *Note that this equation is the mathematical translation for the word problem in Exercise 4.*

BONUS: a. 6, <u>-1</u>, <u>5</u>, 4

       b. 10, <u>-6</u>, <u>4</u>, -2, <u>2</u>, 0

WARM-UP 19

1. 15.5 inches

2. 15.5   *Note that this equation is the mathematical translation for the word problem in Exercise 1.*

3. $n > -5$ *Discuss the result of dividing both sides of an inequality by a negative number.*

4.

1	2	3	4	5	6	10	19
1	4	9	16	25	36	100	361

5. a. 2,500

   b. 500

BONUS: 45 ways. One method is to *Use A Systematic List.*

See WARM-UP 14. There are many more problem-solving strategies than those listed; however, these seem to be the ones used most often in algebra.

WARM-UP 20

1. a. -216

   b. -54

2. True

3. $w = 11$

4. $9n + 8$ *Be certain that students check their results by substituting values for* n.

5. $w = 13$

BONUS:

1st	2nd	3rd	4th	5th	6th	100th	nth
2	6	12	20	30	42	10,100	$n(n + 1)$

WARM-UP 21

1. False; the result is $8n^6$.

2. $3x + 4$

3. $n = 8$

4. 24, 25, 26, 27

5. $n = 24$ *Note that this equation is the mathematical translation for the word problem in Exercise 4.*

BONUS:

Compare these numbers with the rectangular numbers given in WARM-UP 20.

1st	2nd	3rd	4th	5th	6th	100th	nth
1	3	6	10	15	21	5,050	$\dfrac{n(n + 1)}{2}$

WARM-UP 22

1. **a.** False

b. True

c. False

d. True

Be certain that students check their results by substituting values for n.

2. 47, 49, 51, 53

3. $n = 47$

4. $n = 1$

5. $n = \dfrac{1}{2}$

BONUS: 28 games. Several strategies are possible. One method is to *Make A Systematic List.* Suppose the teams are lettered A to H. Then, the games are labeled:

AB BC CD DE EF FG GH
AC BD CE DF EG FH
AD BE CF DG EH
AE BF CG DH
AF BG CH
AG BH
AH

Alternatively, refer to Exercise 3 on WARM-UP 16.

WARM-UP 23

1. $16n^6$

2. 12 inches

3. 5¢

4. Answers will vary. One possibility is:
$3n + 1 = 4n - 2$

Students should be given many opportunities to create problems of their own.

5. $5n^2 + 7n$

BONUS: One method is to use *Guess And Check.*

19 bicycles and 4 tricycles

WARM-UP 24

1. This figure shows that:

$n(n + 2) = n^2 + 2n$

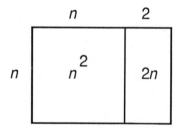

2. Equations will vary. One possibility is: "The sum of the two numbers is 50," in which case the answer is 14.

3. No solution possible

4. Answers will vary. One possibility is:

$2n - 3 = -n + 10 + 3n$

5. 1, 2, 3, 4, 6, 8, 12, 16, 24, 48

BONUS: 13 by 19

WARM-UP 25

1. Information not needed:

Margie's age, her telephone number, the number of years she's been selling papers, and the cost of the papers.

39 papers sold on Sunday

2. n can be any number.

3. Equations will vary. One possibility is:

$-3(n - 1) = 2(n + 2) - (5n + 1)$

4. 1, 2, 4, 8, 16, 32, 64   *Ask students to find other numbers that have an odd number of factors.*

5. $n(2n + 5)$ or $2n^2 + 5n$

BONUS: The last digit is 6. The strategies are *Use Simpler Cases* and *Look For Patterns*. Every fourth number ends in 6.

WARM-UP 26

1. True

2. $2x^2y^2$

3. $(x + 3)(x + 2) = x^2 + 5x + 6$

4. Problems will vary. One possibility is: "The sum of three consecutive even numbers is 66. What are the numbers?" The answers are 20, 22, and 24.

5. $x = 7$

$x = -7$

BONUS: Here are some possibilities:

$0 + (-2) + 6 = 4$

$0 - (-2) + 6 = 8$

$0 + (-2) - 6 = -8$

$0 - (-2) - 6 = -4$

$0 + (-2) \cdot 6 = -12$

$0 \cdot (-2) \cdot (-6) = 0$

$0 \cdot (-2) + 6 = 6$

$0 \cdot 6 + (-2) = -2$

WARM-UP 27

1. $(2x + 1)(x + 2)$

$2x^2 + 5x + 2$

2. n^3

3. One possibility is: "The perimeter of a rectangle is 100 cm. The length is three times the width. What is the width?"

12.5 cm

4. $-8yz$

5. -5

BONUS: One method is to *Eliminate Possibilities.* 1, 6, and 16 *or* 2, 3, and 16

WARM-UP 28

1. b

2. $x^2 + 8x + 15$

3. 8 years old

4. $x = 8$

5. 63

BONUS: $\dfrac{2(n + 3) + 4}{2} - n = 5$

WARM-UP 29

1. $y^2 + y - 20$

2. $n = 22$

3. 22 nickels   *Emphasize that the equation in Exercise 2 is the translation for the word problem in Exercise 3.*

4. $5{,}300{,}000{,}000 = 5.3 \times 10^9$

Emphasize the importance of expressing numbers in scientific notation.

5. -8

BONUS: $\dfrac{(2n + 6 - 18) \cdot 2}{4} + 6 = n$

b.

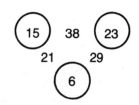

WARM-UP 30

1. $n = 13$ *Emphasize the importance of scientific notation.*

2. 14 dimes *Refer back to the mathematical translation used on a similar problem in WARM-UP 29.*

3. $2x^2 + x - 3$

4. Answers will vary. One possibility is: 0.3, 0.31, 0.32

> *Students will often discover that decimal fractions are easier to use for this type of problem than common fractions, although common fraction answers are certainly acceptable.*

5. $11a - 5b$

BONUS: $\dfrac{(n + 12 - 7) \cdot 3 - 15}{3} = n$

WARM-UP 31

1. False. The correct result is $2.0 \cdot 10^9$.

2. The length is $n + 4$.

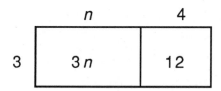

3. 5

4. $n = 4$

5. 4 baseballs at \$2 each. *Note that the equation in Exercise 4 is the translation for the word problem in Exercise 5.*

BONUS:

a.

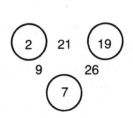

WARM-UP 32

1. $x = 8$

2. 20

3. $5a$

4. 3 hours 20 minutes

5.

1	2	3	4	5	6	100	n
10	21	32	43	54	65	1,099	$11n - 1$

BONUS:

a.

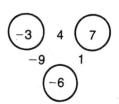

b.

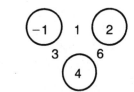

WARM-UP 33

1. Length $= n + 3$
   Width $= n + 2$

2. Length $= n + 4$
   Width $= n + 3$

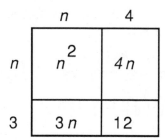

79

3. $t = 4$

4. 4 hours   *Note that the equation in Exercise 3 is the translation for the word problem in Exercise 4.*

5. $n = 2$

BONUS:

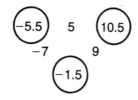

WARM-UP 34

1. $(n - 8)(n - 2)$

2. 1.5 hours

3. 3

4. False

5. $4n + 1$

BONUS: A combination of strategies is possible, including *Use A Drawing, Make A Systematic List,* and *Look For A Pattern.* See WARM-UP 21.

   a. 10

   b. 15

   c. 55

WARM-UP 35

1. False

2. $n = 9$

3. $x = -3, x = 8$

4. $x = -3, x = 8$ *Emphasize that the equation in Exercise 3 is equivalent to the equation in Exercise 4.*

5. 9 trips   *Note that the equation in Exercise 2 is the translation for this problem.*

BONUS: There are 24 possible 3-course meals.

WARM-UP 36

1. Yes, both results are correct.

2. $\dfrac{4}{5}$

3. $\dfrac{1}{3}$ pound

4. $x = 5, x = 2$

5. $(x + 3)(x + 4) = 0$

BONUS:

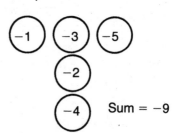

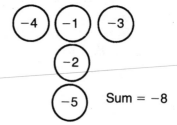

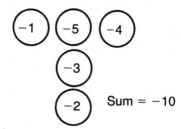

WARM-UP 37

1. $n = 30$

2. Answers will vary. One possibility is to substitute 20 for n.

   The result is $\dfrac{25}{24}$, not $\dfrac{5}{4}$.

3. a. $\dfrac{1}{2}$

   b. The expression cannot be simplified.

4. a. False

   b. True

5. 30   *The equation in Exercise 1 is the translation for this problem.*

BONUS: There is no solution. Note that the sum of three odd numbers is odd and the sum of four odd numbers is even.

WARM-UP 38

1. $\dfrac{1}{3}$

2. $\dfrac{4x}{12}$ $\dfrac{3x}{12}$

3. $\dfrac{7x}{12}$

4.

s	1	2	3	4	5	6	17	20	35
a	1	4	9	16	25	36	289	400	1,225

5. Two angles are $61\frac{2}{3}^{\circ}$ and one angle is $56\frac{2}{3}^{\circ}$. Perhaps a drawing would be helpful.

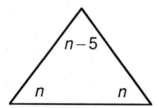

BONUS: $16n + 8$

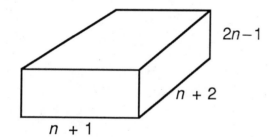

WARM-UP 39

1. $\dfrac{13a}{12}$

2. $\dfrac{b}{3a}$

3.

d	1	2	3	4	10	20	25
c	3.1	6.2	9.3	12.4	31	62	77.5

4. $6x + 2$

5. $2x^2 + x$

BONUS: $\dfrac{1}{100}$

WARM-UP 40

1. $4x + 3x = 84$

2. $x = 12$ *Emphasize that the equations in Exercises 1 and 2 are equivalent.*

3. $\dfrac{2}{3} = \dfrac{6}{9}$ $\dfrac{6}{2} = \dfrac{9}{3}$ $\dfrac{3}{2} = \dfrac{9}{6}$

4.

g	1	2	3	4	5	6	15	30
d	27	54	81	108	135	162	405	810

5. -1

BONUS: $5\frac{1}{2}$ years old

WARM-UP 41

1. $\dfrac{3}{4} = \dfrac{9}{12}$ $\dfrac{3}{9} = \dfrac{4}{12}$

  $\dfrac{4}{3} = \dfrac{12}{9}$ $\dfrac{9}{3} = \dfrac{12}{4}$

2. $\dfrac{7}{8}$ $\dfrac{14}{16}$ $\dfrac{63}{72}$

3. $16x - 6x = 1$

4. $x = \dfrac{1}{10}$

5.

s	1	3	5	10	16
d	$\frac{1}{5}$	$\frac{3}{5}$	1	2	$3\frac{1}{5}$

BONUS: Possibilities include:

  $1 + 2 + 4 = 7$
  $1 \cdot 2 + 4 = 6$
  $2 \cdot (1 + 4) = 10$
  $4 \cdot (1 + 2) = 12$

WARM-UP 42

1.

r	10	20	30	60	80
d	5.5	22	49.5	198	352

2. $4x^2 - 1$

3. $(3x + 1)(3x - 1)$

4. $x = 9$

5. $n = 10$

BONUS: 13 people   *Refer to WARM-UP 16.*

WARM-UP 43

1. $n = 248$

2. 248 words *The equation in Exercise 1 is the mathematical translation of this problem.*

3. a. $a^2 - b^2$

 b. 899

 c. 1,599 *Have students create other multiplication problems that can be done mentally by using this property.*

4.

h	5	10	15	20
c	$4.45	$8.90	$13.35	$17.80

5. $c = \$0.89\,h$

BONUS: 72 scholars

WARM-UP 44

1. 26¼ pounds

2. Problems will vary. One possibility is: "Five tickets cost $21. At this rate, how much will 12 tickets cost?" Answer: $50.40

3.

g	3	6	10	15	20
c	$1.05	$2.10	$3.50	$5.25	$7.00

4. $c = \$0.35g$

5. $n = 25$

BONUS:

A 10-yard by 10-yard pen will provide an area of 100 square yards. This is the largest rectangular pen. A circular pen will provide the greatest area.

w	1	2	3	4	5	6	7	8	9	10
l	19	18	17	16	15	14	13	12	11	10
area	19	36	51	64	75	84	91	96	99	100

WARM-UP 45

1. 26%

2. Answers will vary. One possibility is: "Dead-Eye Joe made 15 out of 16 free throws. What percent is this?" 94%

3. $y < -4$

4. $y > 4$

5. $y = 2.5x$

x	0	2	5	8	10	15
y	0	5	12.5	20	25	37.5

BONUS: One method is to *Work Backwards.*

-1

WARM-UP 46

1. $379.17

2. 4.5 hours   *Note that this problem is not a direct variation.*

3. $b < -2$

4. -6

5. $(10, 8)$

BONUS: There are possibilities other than those listed below.

$$1 = \frac{4 + 4}{4 + 4}$$

$$2 = \frac{4}{4} + \frac{4}{4}$$

$$3 = \frac{4 + 4 + 4}{4}$$

$$4 = \frac{4 - 4}{4} + 4$$

$$5 = (4 \cdot 4 + 4) \div 4$$

$$6 = \frac{4 + 4}{4} + 4$$

$$7 = 4 + 4 - \frac{4}{4}$$

$$8 = 4 + 4 + 4 - 4$$

$$9 = 4 + 4 + \frac{4}{4}$$

$$10 = \frac{4}{0.4} + 4 - 4$$

WARM-UP 47

1. and **2.**

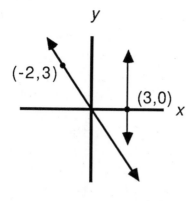

3. a. 4   *Note that the expression simplifies:*
   b. −3
   c. 10
$$\frac{n^2 + n}{n + 1} = \frac{n(n + 1)}{(n + 1)} = n$$

4. $n = 2$

5. $x^2 + 2x + 1$

BONUS: There are three possibilities for both parts of the problem: (13, 5), (7, 13), or (−3, −1).

WARM-UP 48

1. The second clue is not needed.

2. $n = 13, n = −14$

3. a. 4   *Note that the expression simplifies:*
   b. 5
   c. 6
$$\frac{n^2 − 1}{n − 1} = \frac{(n + 1)(n − 1)}{(n − 1)} = n + 1$$

4. 4.5 cm

5. 13 and 14; −14 and −13   *The equation in Exercise 2 is the translation for this problem.*

BONUS: 400 triangles

WARM-UP 49

1. (−3, −4)

2. $n = 4$ or $n = −4$ *Emphasize that the fraction is undefined under these conditions.*

3. $n = \dfrac{10}{9}$

4. $72x^5$

5. 1½ days, if they work at the same rate.   *Note that this problem is not a direct variation.*

BONUS: $78   *Note the triangular number pattern. See WARM-UP 21.*

1st	2nd	3rd	4th	5th	6th
$1	$3	$6	$10	$15	$21

7th	8th	9th	10th	11th	12th
$28	$36	$45	$55	$66	$78

WARM-UP 50

1.

x	0	1	6	11	15	10	12
y	10	9	4	−1	−5	0	−2

2. The graph is a straight line that slopes down from upper left to lower right.

3. $x = −\dfrac{1}{2}$; $x = 5$

4. $x = −\dfrac{1}{2}$; $x = 5$ *The equations in Exercises 3 and 4 are equivalent.*

5. No solution is possible. The world's record for the long jump is less than 30 feet.

BONUS: One method is to *Make A Drawing.*
   a. 9 cubes
   b. 26 cubes

WARM-UP 51

1.

x	−2	−1	0	1	2	3
y	−9	−5	−1	3	7	11

2. The graph is a straight line that slopes rather steeply from lower left to upper right.

3. **c** is correct

4. 10 years old

5. $n = 10$ *This equation is the translation for the problem in Exercise 4.*

BONUS: 28 lines   *See WARM-UP 14.*

WARM-UP 52

1. a. (0,6)

   b. (−3,0)

2. a. It does not cross the *y*-axis.

   b. It does not cross the *x*-axis.

3. Not enough information. Suggest that students make up additional information so that the problem can be solved.

4. $x = 8; x = -3$

5. This equation cannot be solved by factoring. The solutions, in this case, are imaginary numbers.

BONUS: 72 pounds

WARM-UP 53

1. (3, 1)

2. Answers will vary. One possibility is:

   $x = y$ and $x + 2y = 0$

3. $10^1 = 10$

   $10^0 = 1$

   $10^{-1} = 0.1$

   $10^{-2} = 0.01$

   $10^{-3} = 0.001$

4. a. 0.0001

   b. 0.000001

5. $\dfrac{3x + 1}{3}$

BONUS: 10 shots   *This problem can be solved as a "mixture" problem by using this proportion:*

$$\frac{8 + n}{20 + n} = \frac{60}{100}$$

WARM-UP 54

1. Answers will vary. One possible answer is:

   $x + y = 7$

   $x - y = -1$

2. (3, 4)

3. $n = -5$

4. $n = -8$ *This problem shows the results of using scientific notation to multiply 0.0021 by 0.00004.*

5. 13 and 7

BONUS: 9 free throws   *This problem can be solved as a "mixture" problem by using this proportion:*

$$\frac{10}{16 + n} = \frac{40}{100}$$

WARM-UP 55

1. (1,1)

2. $4x + 2y = 6$; yes

3. $n = -1$ *This problem shows the result of using scientific notation.*

4. 1,024

5. 12 and −2

BONUS: 180 inches

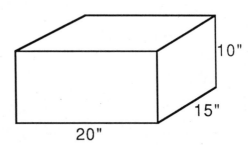

WARM-UP 56

1. There is an infinite number of solutions.

2. The two equations are equivalent and have the same graph. Thus, the intersection is an infinite number of points.

3. a. 0

   b. 5

   c. −5

4. $n = -1$

5. $n = 4$

BONUS: One method is to *Use A Systematic List*.

27 possible ways

Long shots	Field goals	Free throws
5	0	0
4	1	1
4	0	3
3	0	6
3	1	4
3	2	2
3	3	0
2	0	9
2	1	7
2	2	5
2	3	3
2	4	1
1	0	12
1	1	10
1	2	8
1	3	6
1	4	4
1	5	2
1	6	0
0	0	15
0	1	13
0	2	11
0	3	9
0	4	7
0	5	5
0	6	3
0	7	1

WARM-UP 57

1.

C	0	10	20	30	40	50
F	32	50	68	86	104	122

2. A straight line. For every increase of 10 degrees on the Celsius scale there is a corresponding increase of 18 degrees on the Fahrenheit scale.

3. The puzzle problems will vary. One possible puzzle is: "The sum of two numbers is 10. If you add the first number to twice the second number, the result is 8. What are the numbers?"

4. $-16, -8, -4, -2, -1, -\frac{1}{2}, -\frac{1}{4}, -\frac{1}{8}, -\frac{1}{16}$

5. $x > 2$

BONUS: The final result is the original 3-digit number. For example:

$13 \cdot 11 \cdot 7 = 1,001$
$1,001 \cdot 352 = 352,352$
Therefore, $352,352 \div 1,001 = 352$

WARM-UP 58

1.

l	1	2	3	4	6	8	12	24
w	24	12	8	6	4	3	2	1

2. The graph will be a curved line. The graph will never touch either of the axes.

3. $x = 8.5$

4. Area $= 4x^2 + 4x + 1$

   Perimeter $= 8x + 4$

5. $y = 0 \cdot x + (-6)$

BONUS:

$(20 + 2n)(50 + 2n) = 1,000 + 1,800$

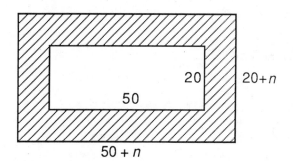

WARM-UP 59

1. $w = 5h - 190$ seems to work best for more people.

2. The result is $x^2 + 6x + 9$.

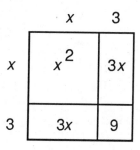

3. $(2x - 3)(x + 1)$

4. $2x - 3$

5. $y = 0$

BONUS: Impossible. She would have to drive infinitely fast.

WARM-UP 60

1. $4r^2 - \pi r^2$ or $r^2 \cdot (4 - \pi)$

2. $y = x^2$ and $xy = 24$

3. $x^3 + 3x^2 + 2x$

4. $x = 0$
   $x = -1$ *Note the similarity between*
   $x = -2$ *Exercises 3 and 4.*

5. $6x^3 + 10x$

BONUS: A combination of strategies are possible, including *Use A Drawing, Make A Systematic List,* and *Look For A Pattern.*
46 cubes

WARM-UP 61

1. $8r^2 - 2\pi r^2$ or $2r^2 \cdot (4 - \pi)$

2. **a.** 7,300
   b. 13,900

3. $y = 5x$

4. The equation cannot be solved by factoring. If the quadratic formula is used, the solutions are:
$$n = \frac{1 \pm \sqrt{17}}{4}$$

5. 456 miles

BONUS: A sum of -1 has the greatest probability of occurring, at 6 out of 36 times.

WARM-UP 62

1. $4r^2 + \pi r^2$ or $r^2 \cdot (4 + \pi)$

2. $y = 2x + \dfrac{7}{2}$

3. **a.** $7x - 1$
   b. $3x + 5$

4. The result is always the number you started with.
$$\frac{2n - 8}{2} + 4 = n$$

5. No solution is possible.

BONUS: $25^2 = 625$
$76^2 = 5{,}776$

WARM-UP 63

1. Line *a.* $y = x + 3$
   Line *b.* $y = x$
   Line *c.* $y = 0 \cdot x + (-3)$

2. 9

3. $x = 4, y = 3$

4. No; her score was 86%.

5. $y = \dfrac{2x}{3} + \dfrac{1}{3}$

BONUS: 21.8 miles

WARM-UP 64

1. Each graph has a *y*-intercept of -3.

2. $x = 0, y = -3$

3. $\dfrac{(x + 2)(x + 1)}{x(x + 1)} = \dfrac{x + 2}{x}$

4. False

5. 32 correct answers

BONUS: $630

WARM-UP 65

1. The formula seems to work reasonably well for people below the age of 21.

2. $x = 1, y = -4$

3. $x = 2, y = 2$

4. $2x^2 + 6x + 5$

5. $n = -1$

BONUS: 9,567
   $+1{,}085$
    10,652

WARM-UP 66

1.

c	60	72	84	96	108
t	52	55	58	61	64

2.

s	1	2	3	4	5
t	50	61	72	83	94

3. Approximately 2.3 inches per minute

4. $-24x^6$

5. -3

BONUS: 3 cats

WARM-UP 67

1.

t	0	1	2	3	4	5
d	0	16	64	144	256	400

2.

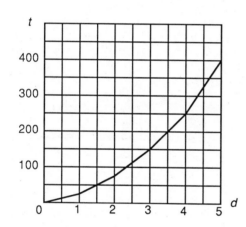

3. Yes

4. $x = \dfrac{y - 39}{11}$

5. $4n$

BONUS: **a.** 4 corner, 10 edge, 4 center
b. 4 corner, 18 edge, 8 center
c. 4 corner, 198 edge, 98 center

WARM-UP 68

1. $(-3,0)$

2. $y = -x + 4$

3. Each graph has a y-intercept of 3.

4. $xy = 12$, and $y = x^2$

5. $(-4,-7)$

BONUS:

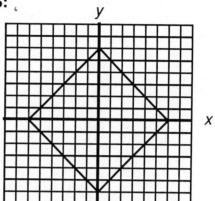

WARM-UP 69

1. $x = 0$

2. $x = -3$

3. $x = \dfrac{1}{5}$

4. $x = -5, x = 3$

5. $x = 7, y = 14$

BONUS: $x = 7.6$

WARM-UP 70

1. $x + (x + 2) + (x + 4) = 255$
The numbers are 83, 85, 87.

2. $20x + 10x = 120$
4 hours

3. $x + 2x + (x + 4) = 80$
19 years old

4. $4x + 3y = 199$
$4x + y = 133$
Cat food costs 25¢ per can.
Dog food costs 33¢ per can.

5. $x + y = 20$
$x - 2y = 14$
The numbers are 2 and 18.

BONUS: 400 watts-heures